# Pickles, Pr



# & Dilemmas

## Situations for Creative Problem Solving

Written by **Dianne Draze**

Illustrated by **Amber Tornquist**

# Contents

**About this Book** . . . . . . . . 3
Problem Solving Behavior . . . . . . . . 3
Pickles and Problem Solving . . . . . . . . 3
Other Uses . . . . . . . . 3
The CPS Process . . . . . . . . 4
**Pickles, Problems & Dilemmas** . . . . . . . . 5 - 32
Warm Ups . . . . . . . . problems 1 - 18
Everyday Situations . . . . . . . . problems 19 - 42
Personal and Interpersonal . . . . . . . . problems 43 - 56
Serious Concerns . . . . . . . . problems 57 - 84

Edited by Sonsie Conroy

ISBN 1-883055-04-0

# About This Book

## Problem-Solving Behavior

This book is about problems, but it is also about how people can become better problem solvers. What do people typically do when they have problems? Some typical behaviors are to:

- ask friends for advice and do whatever they suggest
- worry and stew, sure that any solution will be less than perfect
- just charge forward without really thinking about consequences
- choose the easiest solution.

These actions usually result in solutions that are less than satisfactory. With instruction and practice though, anyone can learn to attack problems in a logical, methodical manner that will produce favorable results.

Teaching students to be good problem solvers is important not only so that they can be fully-functioning individuals in their personal lives, but also so that they can satisfactorily solve problems in the work place and seek creative ways to deal with worldwide predicaments. These are skills that students will use today in dealing with their friends, their families and their immediate needs; but they are also skills that they will heavily rely on when they become the leaders of our businesses and governments. By starting now, students will have many years to practice being competent problem solvers.

## Pickles and Problem Solving

One process that is commonly accepted as an exemplary procedure for solving problems is Creative Problem Solving. This six-step process uses both creative and critical thinking to analyze problems, generate a variety of possible solutions and then select the best solution for implementation. The process is briefly described below, but for a complete teaching guide, Dandy Lion Publications produces two books that teach this process, *Primarily Problem Solving* and *Creative Problem Solving for Kids.*

This book, *Pickles, Problems and Dilemmas*, is a companion for either of the two books on Creative Problem Solving. It presents a selection of problems that range from fun and whimsical to serious and significant. These problems can be used in conjunction with the other two books when you wish to provide students with practice problems. While the end result of teaching problem solving is to provide students with skills that will enable them to select and solve their own problems, there are times during the teaching process when you will want to provide a problem. In these cases, you'll find a delightful selection of problems in this book. Just pick a problem and you've taken the first step to successful problem solving.

## Other Uses

Whether you teach Creative Problem Solving or not, you will find that the situations presented in this book will provide a plethora of thought-provoking material for many classroom learning situations. Some of the other possible applications are:

- **Writing Assignments** - These situations are great for both creative and expository writing. One approach is to give students the situation and ask them to pose a solution and tell why their solution is good. Another approach would be to give students the problem situation and ask them to tell the story behind it; that is, to describe the problem from a personal point of view.
- **Oral Presentations** - Let students choose a problem situation that they find interesting and develop it into a speech by giving background information and posing a solution. They should, in essence, try to sell their solution.
- **Drama** - As a way to understand different points of view, ask groups of students to act out different problem situations, presenting the varying opinions on the topic.
- **Moral Development** - For those problems that pose questions involving values, ask students to tell what they would do. Discuss the consequences of each possible action.

- **Personal Applications** - Ask students to tell about a time they had a similar problem.
- **Brainstorming** - Put up the situation next to a large piece of paper and ask students to write all the possible solutions they can think of.
- **Current Events** - Many of the problems posed toward the end of this book deal with problems of a national or global nature. Ask students to choose a problem situation and develop it into an in-depth research project. They should do all the necessary research on the problem before posing possible solutions.

## The CPS Process

**1. Sensing Problems**

In the first step of CPS, students must select a problem. This step involves identifying a perplexing situation or a problem that needs solving. Usually people have more problems than they know what to do with, so it is a matter of selecting the most pressing problem. If the problems in this book are used, this step is eliminated or streamlined.

**2. Finding Facts**

In this step, students look at both what they already know and what they need to find out. They find all the important, relevant facts that relate to the problem. If not enough information is known, they should ask questions that will result in additional information.

**3. Defining the Problem**

In this step, students look at the problem from several different perspectives and write different "how to" problem statements. The most common way to generate problem statements is to complete the statement "In what ways might I/we..."

**4. Finding Ideas**

After selecting the best problem statement, students then think of many ideas or alternatives to solve the problem. Without analyzing ideas, they try to generate a large number of unusual, unique, creative ideas. Only after they have created a long list do they select those ideas that seem most workable.

**5. Judging Ideas**

In this step, students choose the most useful idea. To do this, they first determine appropriate evaluative criteria. Then they use these criteria to systematically rate each idea. Once all ideas are rated, they look at the ideas and their ratings and try to find the one best solution.

**6. Taking Action**

In the last step of the process, students outline a plan of action for implementing the idea(s) selected. They consider sources of assistance and potential problems. They make a list of short-term and long-term activities.

## 1. FIELD TRIP PERMISSION

You're at school and you realize that today is the day your class is going on a field trip and you forgot your permission slip. You need to think of several plans in case your mother cannot bring the slip to you. You really want to go on the field trip.

## 2. Scratching Post

You just planted a new tree in your back yard. You are proud of your efforts and want the tree to thrive. Your cat, however, is using the tree as a scratching post. You fear that this will eventually kill the tree.

## 3. Dropped Token

You just dropped your one and only bus token down the drainage grate. You need to get it out or you cannot ride the bus home. What can you do?

## 4. Cat Food

Each day you put food out on the back porch for your cat so she can eat while you are at school and your parents are at work. Other animals come into your yard and eat all the food so your cat does not have enough to eat.

## 5. Locked Out

You come home from school and realize that you forgot your key and you are locked out of the house. Your mother is not due home for another hour and it is starting to rain.

## 6. Being Green

You are a prince who has been turned into a frog. The only way you can break the magic spell is to get a princess to kiss you. How can you get the attention of a princess and convince her to kiss you?

## 7. SNOW REMOVAL

It snows quite a bit where you live. You hate to shovel the snow off the sidewalks. What can you do about this situation?

## 8. PROBLEMS UP HIGH

You are the director of public safety. You need to make plans for several possible problems in your city. One problem is getting people out of high rise buildings when there are fires or damage that would prevent them from using the elevators or stairs. What are some ways you could get people down from the top floors?

## 9. Improvements

You work for a company that manufactures one of the following products. Sales have been falling. It is your job to think of ways of improving the product so you can generate more sales.

- spatula
- baseball hat
- pencil
- portable tape player
- bicycle

## 10. *Your Wish*

You got what you wished for and now it is a big problem. What was your wish? What problem has it caused? How can you solve the problem?

## 11. Getting There

You are having a party and have invited 10 friends. You are going to the roller rink 10 miles from your home. Your parents have two cars — one that carries 4 passengers and a driver and one that carries only one passenger and a driver. How can you get all your friends from your house to the roller rink and back again if your parents don't want to leave any of the guests unattended at either location?

## 12. New Pet

You want a pet. You are allergic to fur and your mother is afraid of reptiles and amphibians.

## 13. Stolen Clothes

You are at the beach and while you were out swimming a dog stole your shoes and shirt. Your friends are inside a restaurant waiting for you. You are really hungry and would like to join them, but the sign in the window says, "No Shoes, No Shirt, No Service!" If you cannot go inside the restaurant, what can you do?

## 14. Lost Car Key

You lost your car key and you are 100 miles away from home. What can you do?

## 15. Pet Alligator

When you got Hank, your pet alligator, he was small and cute. Now he has grown quite big and has a voracious appetite. Your parents say you have to come up with a plan to do something with Hank.

## 16. Lost Snake

The police have just been alerted by a young snake owner that his black mamba has escaped and is somewhere in the neighborhood. The snake is very aggressive, very deadly, and can climb trees. As the person who has been put in charge of this problem, what can you do?

## 17. Coaxing a Ground Hog

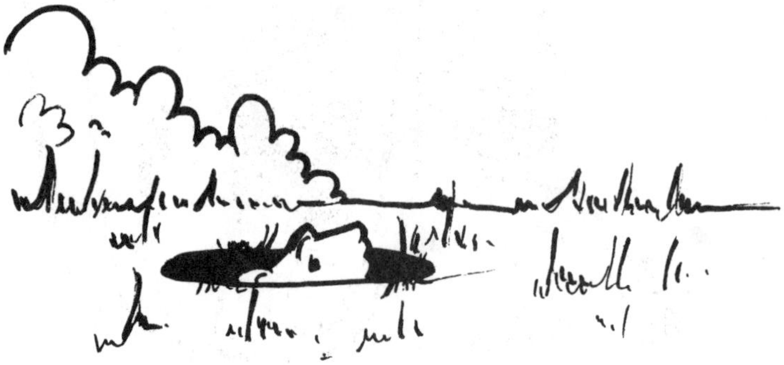

It's Ground Hog Day. All the local media are in your yard to see what will happen when the ground hog comes out of his hole. It's cold and you want to get this procedure over with as soon as possible. How can you coax the ground hog out of his hole?

## 18. *Pirates*

You are an English shipping company owner. Your ships do trading around the world. Lately pirates in the Caribbean have been seizing your boats, stealing the cargo and killing the crews. It is hard to get crews to sail on voyages to this area. What can you do?

## 19. Barking Dog

You just got a new dog and she barks a lot when you leave her home alone. This irritates the older lady who lives across the street. She complains to you often. She says that if you don't do something, she will call Animal Regulation. You are at school most of the day and both of your parents work, so there is no one home for most of each day.

## 20. Broken Refrigerator

Your refrigerator is completely full of food when it stops running. The repair person cannot come until tomorrow. In the meantime, all your food will spoil. What can you do?

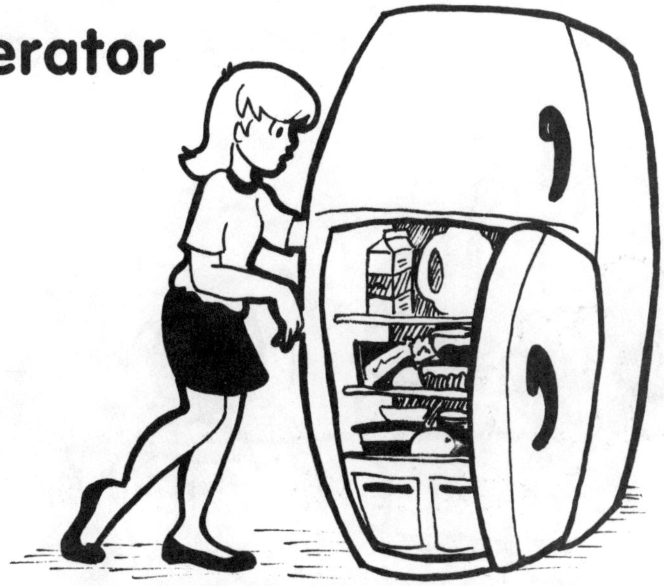

## 21. Ants

EEK! Ants! They are everywhere. You don't mind when they are outside, but you hate it when they invade your house. How can you deal with the ant problem in your house?

## 22. Rained Out

You have a birthday party planned for this afternoon but when you look out the window you see that it is raining. All the party activities (swimming, water slide, treasure hunt) and food (barbecued hamburgers, make-it-yourself sundaes) were planned for outside. What can you do now?

## 23. Late for School

You have trouble waking up each morning and are often late for school. When you are late, you have to make up twice the amount of time during lunch time.

## 24. Eat Your Vegetables

Children often do not like to eat vegetables. Vegetables, however, have many vitamins that are good for people, especially children who are growing. How can you make vegetables more appealing to children?

## 25. Noisy Hobby

You have just taken up playing the drums. You need to practice every day. Your mother says that you cannot practice in the house because you will disturb your family and neighbors.

## 26. Violin or Saxophone?

You want to learn how to play the saxophone. Your parents want you to learn to play the violin because they have a violin left over from when your older sister took lessons. Your sister disliked the violin. You think you will dislike it also.

## 27. Art Supplies

Your school does not have enough money for art supplies. You love art and want to be able to do art in school.

## 28. Sitting on the Bench

You are on the baseball team but the coach never lets you play. You think you will never get to be a better player by sitting on the bench.

## 29. Smoking Grandfather

Your grandfather lives with you. He has smoked nearly all his life and is not likely to quit now. Whenever you are in a room where he is smoking the smoke really irritate you. It makes you very congested. You also feel that smoking is an unhealthy habit.

## 30. Raising Money

Your class has to raise $500 for a class trip. You cannot just ask everyone to bring in a certain amount of money. As a group you need to raise the money.

## 31. Munching Deer

Your family has a lovely garden. You raise vegetables, flowers and fruit. Your problem is that deer come into your garden and eat everything in sight. They even eat your rose bushes and the bark on the trees. If they eat everything, there won't be enough for your family.

## 32. Transportation to School

You live several miles out of town. You take a bus to school and must leave school when the bus leaves in the afternoon. It is difficult for you to get together with your friends or to take part in after-school activities. Both your parents work from 8 a.m. to 5 p.m. each day.

## 33. Improving Cafeteria Food

What's for lunch in the school cafeteria today? Is it good or just so-so? Make a plan for improving the lunches in your cafeteria. Make sure they are nutritious as well as appetizing.

## 34. Water Skiing Party

You have been invited to a water skiing party in 3 weeks. You really want to go, but you are afraid of water. You have never learned how to swim. You really want to go to the party but you don't want the other kids to make fun of you.

## 35. Getting the Teacher's Attention

You are a good student. You usually know all the right answers. You have noticed, though, that the teacher mostly calls on boys. You raise your hand, but you never get called on. The teacher has said that part of your grade is your participation in class activities and discussions. You would like the teacher to know that you understand the material and would like to get credit for participation.

## 36. Dreary Basement

Your parents say you can have a party but you have to have it in the basement. Your basement is a mess and is cold, dark and dank. You don't think it will be a very good place for a party. Your parents don't want the party in the main part of the house because they have all new furniture.

## 37. Future Plans

You are a very good student and want to go to college. Your parents have just informed you that they will not be able to help pay for your college expenses. How can you reach this future goal?

## 38. Land for Youth

Someone has donated 3 acres of land to be used to help the youth in your community. What can you do with this land that will benefit a large number of children?

## 39. Too Much Shade

Your neighbor has a beautiful tree growing in his yard. It is so large that it encroaches into your yard, creating so much shade in one corner of your yard that you cannot get anything to grow. You would like to have a vegetable garden in this corner of your yard. Your neighbor refuses to cut down the tree. He is quite fond of the tree and the shade it provides.

## 40. NEIGHBORHOOD'S PETS

You live in an area where most people have large 2-acre lots. One family in the neighborhood has several animals that cause problems for the other neighbors. The goats make constant noise. The rooster wakes everyone up each morning. The chickens create smells and dust. The horse creates a problem with flies and is always breaking down the fence. What can be done?

## 41. Getting the Word Out

You and your friends are producing a play. You want to inform other people about your production but you don't have much money for advertising. How can you tell other people about your play?

## 42. Vacation Plans

Your parents always go on vacation to their cabin in the mountains. After doing this for years, you think it is boring. You would like to go to the beach instead. Your parents say that they cannot afford to rent a house at the beach.

## 43. STRESSED OUT

You are overbooked. You have so much to do and so little time to just relax. If this is your problem, write down all the facts associated with the problem and then find a solution.

## 44. Sharing the Television

Your family has one television and everyone has to share. It is not unusual for two people to want to watch two different programs at the same time. What are some creative solutions to this common family problem?

## 45. Staying Home

It is estimated that as many as 7 million school-age children must stay home alone after school each day because their mothers and fathers must work and cannot arrange for after-school care. The main activity for these children is watching television. Both teachers and parents agree that the lack of supervision is detrimental. Is this a problem in your community? If so, what can be done about it?

## 46. Counteracting Advertising

Many cereal manufacturers produce enticing commercials aimed at selling their sugar-laden cereals to young children. How can you combat or counteract this strong, appealing message to youngsters?

## 47. SHARING THE NEWSPAPER

Your family gets one newspaper. You need to cut out articles every night for current events at school. Your father wants to read the paper later in the evening, after you are in bed. He does not like reading a paper with holes in it. How will the two of you solve this problem?

## *48. SHARING THE WORK*

You are working on a group project and one person in the group does not do her share of the work. Everyone will get the same grade on the project.

## 49. Messy Friend

Your friend comes over to your house to visit and always makes a big mess in your room. After she leaves, you usually get in trouble and have to clean it up. You don't think this is fair. You really like your friend and want to continue seeing her but you're tired of cleaning up after her.

## 50. Borrowing Library Books

A friend always borrows your library books and then forgets to return them so you have to pay the fine. The friend never offers to pay the past-due fine.

## 51. Being Included

You hang out with three friends. Sometimes they do things and forget to invite you. You are not sure if they do this on purpose or if you just get overlooked. It hurts your feelings.

## 52. Bossy Classmate

Your classroom uses cooperative work groups. There is one person in your group who is very pushy and vocal. He always leads the group into doing the project wrong or getting the wrong answer. You know that the answers are wrong, but you are not as forceful as he is. You hate to get a bad grade, but you are afraid that he will just ridicule you if you speak up and contradict him.

## 53. A Dishonest Dare

You are at the mall with your friends. They dare you to steal something from a store. You know that it is wrong and you will get in a lot of trouble at home if you are caught. You don't, however, want to appear cowardly in front of your friends.

## 54. TEASING

The kids in your classroom make fun of your name. They are always turning it into a rhyme. This makes you feel both angry and embarrassed. What can you do?

# 55. New Friend

You have become friends with someone your other friends do not like. This new friend is really nice and fun to be with, but your other friends don't want to give her a chance because they say she is too weird. While she does not care for personal appearances and has a few odd habits, you do not want to give up this new friendship just to please your old friends.

# 56. One-Sided Friendship

You feel like a dumping ground. Everyone comes to you and tells you their problems. They trust your advice. When you want to talk about your problems, they ignore you or quickly change the conversation back to their problems. You have problems that you would like to discuss with your peers.

# 57. SEXUAL HARASSMENT

A boy who sits in back of you makes rude, sexually-oriented comments to you during class. What can be done about this one isolated situation or about sexual harassment among people your age in general?

## 58. Smoking

Smoking is the primary nongenetic contributor to death in the U.S. Although the number of adults who are taking up smoking has dropped, the number of teenagers who have begun to smoke has been rising steadily. What are some ideas for reversing this trend?

## 59. Garbage Dump

There is a vacant lot next to your school. People are always bringing their garbage to this area and dumping it. What can be done to discourage people from dumping their garbage here and make it an attractive area?

## 60. Traffic Accidents

The leading cause of death for young people between the ages of 16 and 25 is traffic accidents. Find additional statistics for this situation for both the nation and your local community and then decide what can be done about this problem.

## 61. Improving Your Community

Your city is giving grants of up to $25,000 to members of the community for projects that will solve social or environmental problems. The city will put up half of the money and the other half has be donated by community members. The community portion may be in the form of labor and materials rather than cash. Investigate various problems in your community and make a proposal for a grant.

## 62. Drugs

Drug use and sales has become a problem in many communities. The violence that is associated with drug sales endangers people who live in neighborhoods with high drug trafficking. The cost to the federal government for controlling drugs has risen from 1.5 million dollars in 1981 to close to 13 million dollars in 1993. Research this problem and pose a solution.

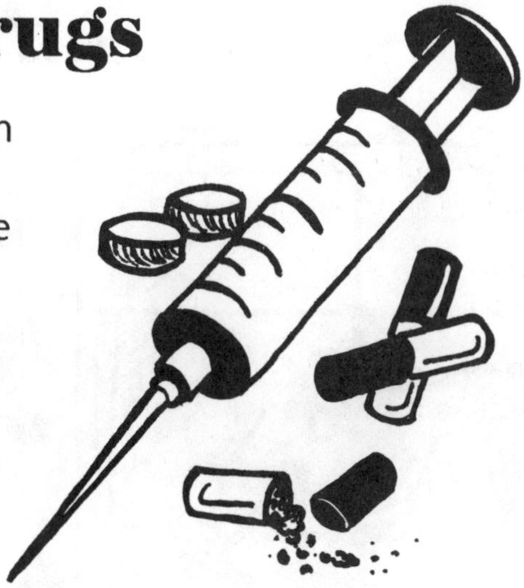

## 63. Wind Power

In some windy areas, you can find windmill farms where thousands of windmills catch the wind and turn it into power. One problem is that the spinning propellers on the windmills kill many birds that are flying in the area. With a decrease in birds, there is an increase in rodents and insects. How can you use these power sources without killing birds and in the process increasing the number of rodents that carry diseases and the number of insects that prey on surrounding crops?

## 64. Gun Ownership

The increase in gun ownership and use in our country causes many people to be concerned. In particular, weapons that are brought to school pose a serious threat to the welfare of all students in the school. Homocide is now the third largest killer of children in our country. Survey information about this problem in our country and also in your community. Pose a solution.

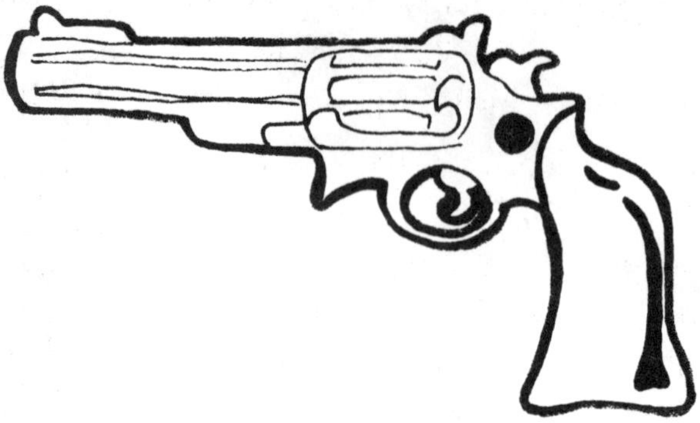

## 65. Air Pollution

Air pollution is so bad in many communities that children are not allowed to go outside for recess for many days during the school year. More than one third of Americans live in areas where pollution exceeds acceptable levels. The decline in air quality creates significant health problems. What would you suggest doing about this problem?

## 66. Graffiti

Neighborhoods in many large cities are covered with graffiti. The people who paint the graffiti on the walls and fences consider it a form of art as well as a way to mark territory. Homeowners and business owners consider it a destruction of their property. What can be done?

## 67. DESERTED AREAS

In many cities you can find small shopping malls or building complexes that have been deserted as businesses move to other locations. Once a couple of businesses move out, the others follow. Finally these buildings are boarded up. They are worse than useless; they are ugly and often dangerous. Find someplace like this in your community and make a plan to solve the problem.

## 68. Getting Exercise

According to the Center for Disease Control, 30% of the people in our country get no exercise. Those who do exercise do not get enough exercise. Adults typically spend less than three 20-minutes sessions a week at physical activity. This sedentary life poses a greater threat to cardiovascular disease than either smoking or obesity. Find out more information about this situation and pose a solution.

## 69. Media Violence

Many people feel that television programming for young children is too violent. They feel that this violence is unnecessary and detrimental. People in the entertainment industry, on the other hand, feel that any regulation of programming is an infringement on free speech. Find information on this topic from several different sources and then pose a solution.

# 70. Play Places

In many cities, children do not have anywhere that they can play. Either they do not have playgrounds or the playgrounds are not safe. Where do children in your community go to play that they can be safe and have fun? If you don't have a place, make a plan for a place in your neighborhood where children can play.

# 71. Litter

Litter, litter, everywhere! You find it in the classroom, on the playground, beside the road and in the park. Pinpoint the location and sources of litter in your community. How can you solve this problem?

# 72. *Informing Youth*

Young people need information about a lot of subjects that pose possible health hazards for them. These subjects include good nutrition, substance abuse, and AIDS. Choose a subject that you feel people your age do not have adequate information about. Devise a plan to get the information to them in a way that will be factual but also interesting.

# 73. ANIMAL SHELTERS

An astonishingly large number of animals are euthanized each year (8 - 10 million in the U.S. in 1992) in animal shelters because the shelters do not have room for the animals or they need to curb the spread of disease among sheltered animals. Shelters usually house animals only 72 hours before they euthanize them. One third of the dogs in shelters are purebreds. Find out what the statistics are for your area. Make a plan to solve this problem.

# 74. Illiteracy

An astonishing number of adults cannot read. Most of these people have gone to school and even graduated, but they are essentially illiterate. This causes a lot of problems for these people. They would probably be more productive workers and more active citizens if they could read. What can be done about this problem?

# 75. Recycling

In an effort to reduce garbage, many people in our country now recycle many types of garbage. This has created a new problem. There is now more garbage waiting to be recycled than there is a demand for products made out of recycled or reprocessed materials. If you were in charge of this problem, what would you do?

## 76. Acid Rain

Your country is adjacent to a country that has a lot of manufacturing and produces a lot of acid rain. This form of pollution drifts over the border and is killing your forests and destroying buildings and monuments. The other country is not interested in curtailing the manufacturing because it will mean less profits for the company owners and less taxes for the government. What can you do about this very serious problem?

## 77. Hostile Takeover

Your country is south of a hostile country that is always crossing the river that serves as a border and fighting with the people who live in this area, stealing their possessions and destroying their crops. They have done this for many years. You have heard from neighboring countries that this country wants to expand its power and wealth. It has just taken over the country on its northern border. How can you stop this country from taking over your country?

## 78. Hostages

The government of a foreign country has taken 10 people from your country hostage. They won't release the hostages until your country releases two people who are being held awaiting trial for crimes that have taken hundreds of lives. You know that if you release your two hostages, they will take part in acts of terrorism again, if not against your country, against countries with whom you are friends.

## 79. World Hunger

Worldwide an amazing number of people go to bed hungry each night. Even in America a large number of people go hungry. This problem is especially significant for elderly citizens. Research this problem either on a world, national or local level and propose a plan to deal with it.

## 80. School Problem

What problems exist on your playground or school campus? Spend some time analyzing the problems that exist. Then devise a plan to solve one of these problems and improve your school.

## 81. Racism

What things indicate that there may be racism in your school or community? If this is a problem, find a solution.

# 82. Homelessness

The number of people who are without homes has become an increasing problem in our country.  Homelessness affects a wide range of people, including families and their children. There are several causes of this problem, including a decrease in funds for low-income housing. Study this problem in your community and propose a solution.

# 83. Dropouts

On average, about 30 percent of the students in our schools drop out before graduating. This figure is higher in some urban areas. Even with a high school diploma it is not easy to get a decent job; without a diploma it is almost impossible. This problem not only affects individuals, it creates a shortage of skilled workers, which is a drain on economic growth. How would you solve this problem?

# 84. Garbage

In this country we produce about 180 million tons of garbage every year. We produce more garbage per capita than any other country in the world. While the garbage of other countries is largely biodegradable, ours is full of non-biodegradable products as well as materials that are toxic or carcinogenic. On a local level, what can you do about this problem?